Celebrate!

China

Robyn Hardyman

CHELSEA CLUBHOUSE
An Imprint of Chelsea House Publishers

Chelsea Clubhouse
An imprint of Chelsea House
132 West 31st Street
New York, NY 10001

Library of Congress Cataloging-in-Publication Data

Hardyman, Robyn.
  Celebrate China / Robyn Hardyman. — 1st ed.
    p. cm.
  Includes bibliographical references and index.
  ISBN 978-1-60413-270-0
  1. China—Juvenile literature. I. Title.
DS706.H368 2009
  951—dc22
                    2008032572

Chelsea Clubhouse books are available at special discounts when purchased in bulk quantities for businesses, associations, institutions, or sales promotions. Please call our Special Sales Department in New York at (212) 967-8800 or (800) 322-8755.

You can find Chelsea House on the World Wide Web at
http://www.chelseahouse.com

Printed and bound in China

10 9 8 7 6 5 4 3 2 1

This book is printed on acid-free paper.

All links and Web addresses were checked and verified to be correct at the time of publication. Because of the dynamic nature of the Web, some addresses and links may have changed since publication and may no longer be valid.

For The Brown Reference Group Ltd.
Project Editor: Sarah Eason
Designer: Paul Myerscough
Picture Researcher: Maria Joannou
Indexer: Claire Throp
Design Manager: David Poole
Managing Editor: Miranda Smith
Editorial Director: Lindsey Lowe

Consultant Editor
Peter Lewis
Writer and Editor for the American Geographical Society, New York

Author
Robyn Hardyman

Contents

Welcome to China

China has the highest population of any country in the world. Its rich history goes back nearly 4,000 years. Today, China's economy is growing fast and life is changing there.

Russia
Kazakhstan
Kyrgyzstan
Mongolia
North Korea
Tajikistan
Afghanistan
Pakistan
China
Nepal Bhutan
India
Vietnam
Myanmar
Laos

China

China is divided into twenty-two provinces, the islands of Hong Kong and Macau, and four city regions (Beijing, Shanghai, Chongqing, and Tianjin). There are also five **autonomous regions**. China became known as the People's Republic of China following the defeat of the Nationalist government by the Chinese Communist Party in 1949. The Chinese Communist Party has ruled the country ever since. It is the largest political party in the world.

Shenzhen

Shenzhen was once a small fishing village, but in the 1970s it was chosen as one of China's new Special Economic Zones. A lot of money was spent on developing Shenzhen, and it is now one of the fastest growing cities in the world. It is also the busiest port in China, after Shanghai.

Chinese borders

Many countries share a border with China. They include North Korea, Russia, Mongolia, Kazakhstan, Kyrgyzstan, Tajikistan, Afghanistan, Pakistan, India, Nepal, Bhutan, Myanmar (Burma), Laos, and Vietnam. China also has thousands of offshore islands, including Hong Kong and Macau.

CHINESE FACTS

FULL NAME	People's Republic of China
CAPITAL CITY	Beijing
AREA	3.7 million square miles
POPULATION IN 2008	1.33 billion
MAIN LANGUAGE	Chinese Mandarin
MAIN RELIGIONS	Confucianism, Buddhism, Taoism, Islam, Christianity
CURRENCY	Yuan

Great Wall of China

The Great Wall of China is probably the country's most famous structure. It was built to keep out invaders from the north, and the first part of it was erected between 221 and 210 B.C.E. by China's first emperor, Qin Shihuangdi. This great building project was not completed until the fifteenth century C.E. The Great Wall stretches across the north of China for almost 4,000 miles, from the Gobi Desert to the sea. Its twisting route is often compared to the body of a dragon.

Wildlife

The giant panda lives only in the mountains of southwest China. It is now endangered. The bamboo forests where it feeds are being cleared for housing for people.

History Highlights

The Chinese civilization is one of the oldest in the world. Important inventions originated in China long before they reached the West. The Chinese developed a calendar, writing, paper, printing, and the wheel. They also invented gunpowder.

China's ruling dynasties

Dynasty	Date
Xia	about 2000 B.C.E.
Shang	about 1500 B.C.E.
Zhou	about 1030 B.C.E.
Qin	221–205 B.C.E.
Han	206–219 B.C.E.
Time of the three kingdoms	220–580 C.E.
Sui	580–617 C.E.
Tang	618–906 C.E.
Five dynasties	907–959 C.E.
Song	960–1259
Yuan	1279–1367
Ming	1368–1643
Qing	1644–1911
Nationalist republic	1912–1948
People's Republic	1949–present

From about 2000 B.C.E. until the twentieth century C.E., China was ruled by a series of **dynasties** (see box left). Each dynasty was named after the ruling family. During the Zhou dynasty, the influential thinker called Confucius lived and worked. His ideas on the importance of respect for family, school, and the nation are still valued in China today. China was first united as a single nation during the Qin dynasty. The first emperor was Qin Shihuangdi (see box top right). The next dynasty, the Han, lasted four hundred years. At this time, the **Silk Road** was opened up. This was a long trade route from China to the West.

Bronze work

During the Shang dynasty, objects such as this pot were made in **bronze** for the first time.

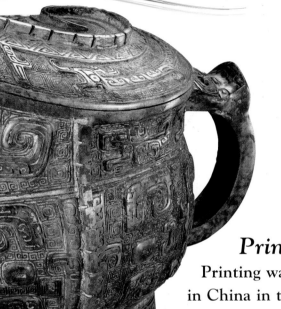

Qin Shihuangdi

Qin Shihuangdi (259–210 B.C.E.) was China's first emperor. He was very ambitious. In 213 B.C.E. he burned almost all the existing books in China, to break all links with the past. He wanted to make China great, and ordered the Great Wall to be built.

Printing

Printing was invented in China in the sixth century B.C.E. and their first books date back to the ninth century C.E. Chinese characters (letters) were carved in reverse into blocks of wood, which were covered with ink. The inked block was then pressed onto paper.

WEB LINKS

To find out more about the terracotta warriors in the tomb of Emperor Qin Shihuangdi visit:
http://www.terracottawarriors.co.uk/

Terracotta warriors

More than 8,000 lifesized **terracotta** warriors were buried in the tomb of Qin Shihuangdi. The face of each one is different. The tomb was discovered in 1974.

Powerful dynasties

During the Tang and Song dynasties, China ruled over much of Central and Southeast Asia. Then, fierce Mongols from the north, led by Genghis Khan (below) conquered the country to set up the Yuan dynasty. Khan's grandson was Kublai Khan, the most famous Yuan emperor. In 1368, the Yuan were defeated by the Chinese Ming dynasty. Their long period of rule was a time of stability. In 1557, some Portuguese traders settled in Macau, and with other Europeans tried to convert the Chinese to Christianity.

A new republic

During the mid-seventeenth century, the Manchus invaded from the north and founded the Qing dynasty. They ruled China until 1911, but Europeans had already taken control of important Chinese ports such as Guangzhou and Hong Kong. The Chinese people became unhappy with their rulers, and in 1911 a rebellion led by Sun Yixian overthrew the emperor and declared China a **republic**.

DID YOU KNOW?
The last emperor was only six years old when he gave up his throne in 1912. He died working as a gardener in 1967.

Jiang Jieshi

The Nationalist Party, led by Jiang Jieshi, fought Mao Zedong's Communist Party for control of China during a long civil war. In 1949, the Communists won and Mao set up the People's Republic of China. Jiang Jieshi fled to Taiwan.

Mao Zedong

In 1949, Mao Zedong (1893–1976) was one of the founders of the People's Republic of China. In 1966, Mao began the **"Cultural Revolution."** Hundreds of thousands of people in middle-class professions such as doctors and lawyers were killed. "Chairman" Mao's tight control over every aspect of life ended when he died in 1976. China then began to open up to the world a bit more, and to allow more businesses to grow. Although China is still not a **democracy**, its economy is growing very rapidly.

Little red books

These books are copies of "Chairman" Mao's famous "Little Red Book." The book contained quotations from his speeches, and Mao expected Chinese people to carry a copy at all times.

A nation of car owners

China is becoming a country of car owners. In 2006, China became the world's second biggest market for vehicles, after the United States. Car sales were 37 percent higher than in 2005, at 3.8 million units.

Fly the Flag

China's flag does not have a long history. It was designed in 1949 by Zeng Liansong, and was the winning entry in a competition to find a flag for the new People's Republic of China. The flag is called the "five-starred red flag." The color red symbolizes the revolution. The large star represents the governing Communist Party. The four smaller stars represent the Chinese people.

China's new flag was officially unveiled in Beijing's Tiananmen Square on October 1st, 1949. To celebrate the **communist** country's fiftieth anniversary in 1999, government officials told all residents to display China's flag. Any people with old or dirty flags were ordered to buy a new one.

Hong Kong and Macau

These are the flags of Hong Kong (top) and Macau (bottom). Hong Kong used to be ruled by Great Britain and Macau used to be ruled by Portugal, but sovereignty of the territories was transferred back to China at the end of the 1990s. Hong Kong and Macau are known as Special Administrative Regions because they are allowed to rule themselves to a large extent.

National emblem

The national emblem of China shows Tiananmen Gate, the entrance to the Forbidden City in Beijing, in a red circle. Above it are the five stars found on the national flag. In the outer circle are sheaves of wheat representing agriculture, and a cog wheel representing industry. It was adopted as the national emblem in 1950.

 Try this!

Make a Chinese dragon bandana

- *The dragon is a respected symbol in China, and red is the luckiest color. Make this dragon bandana to keep you cool on a hot day.*
- *Take a large square white handkerchief and some cardboard. Cut a square out of the cardboard that is about 2 inches smaller than the handkerchief. Stick it onto the center of the handkerchief with double-sided tape.*
- *Mix up some watery red paint, and splash it loosely over the areas of the handkerchief that are showing. When the paint is dry, remove the cardboard. Drizzle some paint in the center.*
- *Draw a Chinese dragon in the center of the handkerchief and paint it black.*
- *Finally, draw some Chinese characters in thick black pen around the edges of your bandana.*

Hymn to China

China's national anthem was originally called "The March of the Volunteers." The words were by Tian Han, and the music was set by Nie Er in 1935. The song became the theme tune of a hit film called **Sons and Daughters of the Storm.** *The film was about the men who fought the Japanese invaders in northeast China in the 1930s. This powerful song expressed the Chinese people's determination to defend their country. In 1949 it was decided that it would be the national anthem of the new People's Republic of China.*

Performing live

The national anthem is performed by the Chinese People's Liberation Army Band at a meeting of the National People's Congress. This is China's legislative body (the group that makes the laws).

CHINA

JAPAN

Fujisawa

The composer of China's national anthem led a very interesting life. Nie Er was a gifted musician who became a movie star at a young age. In 1933, he became a Communist Party member and a secret agent, fighting against Nationalist forces. In 1935, many Communists were arrested and Nie Er fled to the safety of neighboring Japan. Shortly afterward, in 1935, he drowned at a beach in Fujisawa, at the age of twenty-three.

Hand on heart

The Chinese national soccer team sings their national anthem before an international match in 2007.

Translation

The lyrics of the national anthem are translated below.

Arise, ye who refuse to be slaves;
With our very flesh and blood
Let us build our new Great Wall!
The peoples of China are at their most critical time,
Everybody must roar defiance.
Arise! Arise! Arise!
Millions of hearts with one mind
Brave the enemy's gunfire,
March on!
Brave the enemy's gunfire,
March on! March on!
March on, on!

WEB LINKS ▼▼▼▼▼▼▼
To listen to China's national anthem go to:
http://www.national-anthems.net/CH

Regions of China

China is a huge country. It is only slightly smaller than the United States. As a result, its landscape and its climate vary enormously from one area to another.

In the west and south of China is the Tibetan **plateau**. This is an enormous area of rugged terrain. To the east are the lowland plains. China's two great rivers, the Huang He and the Chang Jiang, flow through these from west to east and out to the sea. The land on these plains is the most fertile for growing crops. This is also where most of the population lives. China also has large desert areas, the Taklimakan Desert and the Gobi Desert in the northwest.

Highest railway

Tibet is sometimes called "the roof of the world." In 2006 the world's highest railway opened. It connected Tibet with Qinghai in eastern China by rail for the first time.

CHINESE FACTS

LONGEST RIVERS	*Huang He, about 3,400 miles; Chang Jiang, about 3,900 miles*
HIGHEST MOUNTAIN	*K2 in Himalayas 28,251 feet*
LARGEST CITIES	*Shanghai, Beijing, Guangzhou*

Gobi Desert

The Gobi Desert is so far north that in winter temperatures can fall to −40°F. It is still a desert, however, because it has very low rainfall.

Climate

In the north, winters are incredibly cold and the summers are warm. There is not much rainfall. The south has a tropical climate with warm winters and hot, wet summers.

Three Gorges Dam

A huge new dam is being built on the Chang Jiang River. When finished in 2009, the Three Gorges Dam will be the world's largest hydroelectric dam.

Quake!

China is hard hit from very strong earthquakes. In May 2008, a severe earthquake hit Sichuan province, killing and injuring tens of thousands of people.

What's Cooking?

Food is a central part of Chinese culture. Chinese cuisine varies considerably from one region to another, but there are two main kinds of cooking: Cantonese food comes from the north, east, and south; and Sichuan food comes from the central and southwestern regions.

Cantonese food is typically steamed, boiled, or stir-fried. This is a healthy way of cooking, because it uses very little fat. The main ingredients of this type of Chinese food are seafood, pork, chicken, and vegetables. Dishes are stir-fried in a wok, a large, round-bottomed pan that is held over a strong flame. Rice and vegetables are steamed in containers made of bamboo. These stack on top of each other, over one pan of boiling water.

Dim sum

Dim sum are small, steamed dumplings filled with meat, vegetables, or seafood. They are popular served with tea. They are a typical midday meal and are usually served in a small basket or on a small plate.

Sichuan food

Sichuan cooking uses more chili, so some of the dishes are very hot and spicy. One famous Sichuan dish is *kung po* chicken, which is chicken fried with peanuts and chili pepper.

Buffet meals

Chinese meals are not served in courses. Most of the dishes are put on the table at the same time, and people take small amounts of each one in turn into their own bowl.

What's on the menu?

A typical meal is shown below.

Steamed scallops in their shells

Deep fried seaweed

Seafood with vegetable and bean curd soup

Shredded beef with chili sauce

Steamed fish with garlic, spring onions, and ginger

Stir fried vegetables

Boiled rice

Egg fried rice

Noodles with beansprouts

Lychees

Tea

Try this!

Let's make Chinese chicken noodle soup

Ingredients:

chicken stock, made with 1½ pints
   hot water
2 tablespoons soy sauce
1 tablespoon sesame oil
2 oz fine egg noodles
4 oz shiitake mushrooms, halved
cooked chicken breast, shredded
2 oz young leaf spinach
1 red chili, deseeded and finely shredded

Heat the stock, soy sauce, and sesame oil in a saucepan and bring to a boil. Add the egg noodles and mushrooms to the pan, and simmer for two minutes. Add the shredded chicken and the spinach, and heat through for a few more minutes. Ladle the broth into bowls, scatter with the shredded chili, and serve. For a vegetarian version, you can replace the chicken with more vegetables, such as finely chopped cabbage and spring onions.

How Do I Say...?

There are fifty-six different ethnic groups in China, and each one has its own language and traditions. By far the biggest group is the Han Chinese, who make up more than 90 percent of the Chinese people. The largest of the smaller groups are the Mongols, Uyghurs, Tibetans, and Miao.

Mandarin is the most commonly spoken language in modern China, and everyone learns it in school. It is spoken by more than one billion people. Wú is spoken in the far east of China, around Hong Kong and Shanghai, by about seventy-seven million people. Cantonese is spoken by about sixty million people in the far south and in Hong Kong and Macau. Westerners find it difficult to speak Mandarin, as the meaning of a word can alter with just a small change in pronunciation.

Words and phrases

English	Mandarin	How to say it
hello	ni hao	nee-how
goodbye	zaijian	zy-see-an
thank you	xiexie	see-ah see-ah
my name is ...	wo jiao ...	woe see-ow
how are you?	ni hao ma?	nee-how mar

Symbols

As a written language, Chinese has been used for 6,000 years. It does not have an alphabet, but uses symbols called characters to represent words. Some words have one character, others have several. There are more than 50,000 characters. The one shown left means "dragon." All Chinese dialects use the same characters, but they pronounce them in different ways.

DID YOU KNOW?

An ethnic group known as the Miao people live in southern China. The Miao are divided into smaller groups. They speak several dialects and have different customs. The Yi also live in rural areas of southern China. They speak Yi, a language similar to Burmese. The Hui live in northwest China. They are mostly Muslims. The Buyei live in the high-altitude forests of Guizhou province, as well as in Yunnan and Sichuan provinces. They speak the Buyei language.

Chinese proverbs

Chinese thinkers have always been seen as a source of wisdom. Some of these Chinese proverbs and sayings come from written sources, others have been passed down the generations by word of mouth.

"A child's life is like a piece of paper on which every person leaves a mark."

"To know the road ahead, ask those coming back."

"It is better to light a candle than to curse the darkness."

"He who asks is a fool for five minutes, but he who does not ask remains a fool forever."

Emotional characters

These characters (right) are similar if you look closely. The one at the top means "love," but without the top of the character it means "friend" as shown below.

WEB LINKS

Find more Chinese proverbs at:
http://www.famous-proverbs.com/chinese.htm

Stories and Legends

China's culture includes many legends and stories. Some are about the creation of the world and some are about the origins of China. Others are about mythical creatures and heroic people.

The tale of Chang'e

Chang'e and her husband Houyi were immortals **banished to Earth as mortals.** Houyi went to find the pill that would let them become immortal again. He found it and carried it home to share, but Chang'e swallowed the whole pill for herself. She floated up into the sky (shown in this painting) and landed on the Moon, where she still lives with a rabbit for company.

The dragon is one of the most important creatures in all of Chinese mythology. It is still deeply respected today as a powerful animal, and it is disrespectful to disfigure its image in any way. The dragon is a symbol of strength, goodness, courage, and endurance. There are nine different types of Chinese dragons. One is believed to control all waters, so people pray to it to bring rain. Another dragon guards the house of the gods, and a third was the symbol of the emperors. During the late Qing dynasty, the dragon was even shown on the national flag. Dragons are called *long* in Chinese.

DID YOU KNOW?
In 2007, China named its first lunar probe "Chang'e 1," in honor of the goddess from the legend.

Without wings

Chinese dragons have snakelike bodies, four legs, and do not usually have wings. Most pictures of Chinese dragons show them playing with a flaming pearl. Legend says that the pearl gives them their power, and allows them to ascend into heaven.

Water monkey

The water monkey is a mythical creature. It lives in one of China's many lakes, and people believe it likes to drag victims under the water.

The Legend of the Carp

"The Legend of the Carp" says that a carp (a large fish) that is able to leap over the mythical Dragon Gate will become a dragon. Many people have looked for the location of this Gate, but no one has found it. Several waterfalls in China are believed to be the right place. This legend is designed to teach people about the effort that is needed to overcome obstacles in life.

Fenghuang

Fenghuang is a Chinese mythical bird that rules over all other birds. It is a powerful symbol of great virtue. It appears in peaceful and prosperous times, but hides when trouble is near.

Art and Culture

China's long history has produced a wonderfully rich cultural history. The different regions of this large country enjoy a magnificent variety of artistic traditions.

China has been producing beautiful pots, vases, and bowls for thousands of years. The Chinese invented a kind of pottery called porcelain. This is very fine and fragile. They painted their porcelain with creatures and flowers, or with stories from the past.

Opera
Chinese opera dates from the Sung dynasty. There are different kinds of opera in different regions. One of the most popular is Beijing opera. The operas tell traditional stories, and can include mime, dance, acrobatics, and fencing, as well as drama and singing.

Painting

Chinese paintings are made with brushes and inks, rather than paints. Traditionally they are made on paper and silk, which are then mounted on scrolls, which can be hung or rolled up. Landscapes are a particularly popular subject.

Ming vase

The Ming period (1368–1643) produced beautiful porcelain, such as this bowl. The famous blue and white Ming style was made using an underglaze of cobalt blue pigment imported from the Middle East.

Calligraphy

In China, writing has become an art form in its own right, called **calligraphy**. Children are taught to create beautiful characters from an early age. They use special brushes and ink.

Remarkable buildings

The Potala Palace is in Lhasa, the capital of the region of Tibet. This amazing building, perched on a hillside, has 1,000 rooms. It was built in the seventeenth century for Tibet's spiritual leader, the Dalai Lama. The current Dalai Lama now lives in exile abroad.

Make Your Own Fortune Cookies

These cookies have pieces of paper inside with messages on them, so you can give them to your friends and family at parties and celebrations.

Fortune cookies were first invented by Chinese **immigrants** in the United States. Although fortune cookies are often served in Chinese restaurants as a dessert, they are not commonly used in the People's Republic of China.

1 On the rice paper, use a pencil and compass to draw circles that are about 4 inches across. Cut out the rice paper circles with scissors.

2 Fold a rice paper circle in half. Use the hole punch to make four holes around the open edge. This will make eight holes in all, because the circles are folded in half.

3 Write your special message on a small piece of paper and slip it carefully inside the cookie.

24

DID YOU KNOW?

Fortune cookie messages are often smart sayings. Try making up your own phrases for fun. Have you heard any of these wise words before?

- A friend asks only for your time, not for your money.
- A journey of a thousand miles begins with a single step.
- Distant water does not put out a fire.
- A member of your family will do something that will make you proud.

4 Use a strawberry lace to lace the cookie closed. Tie together the ends of the lace.

5 Stick on small candies with the icing. You can make faces or other patterns with them. Add extra decorations with the writing icing. Give the fortune cookies to your friends and family. Enjoy!

Ready-made cookies

Fortune cookies that you can buy are made from flour, sugar, butter, milk, and vanilla. The crisp, sweet cookies are folded around the "fortune" message inside.

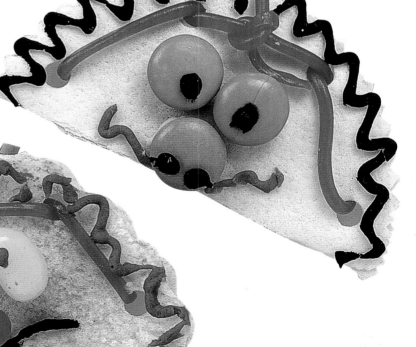

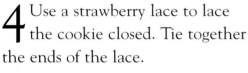

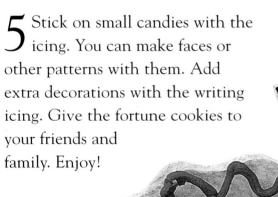

Sports and Leisure

Chinese people work hard. About two thirds of the population lives in the countryside, working the land and keeping animals. People in the cities work hard, too, but they may have more time and money to enjoy their leisure time.

VALENCIA 2008

The most popular traditional sports in China are **martial arts** such as *Tai Chi* and *Kung Fu*. Tai Chi involves a series of slow, controlled body movements. Kung Fu is a method of self-defense. It involves sharp blows and kicks to specific points on the opponent's body.

Tai Chi

Many people like to do *Tai Chi* in the early morning, as part of a group. They exercise in parks or other open spaces. It prepares them well for the day ahead.

Way to go!

There are more than 300 million bicycles in China! They are the most popular way to get around in the cities.

Modern sports

People love to play basketball, tennis, and table tennis, and to do gymnastics. The Chinese love to watch sports too. Soccer is the most popular spectator sport.

Liu Xiang

Liu Xiang (born 1983) is a champion Chinese athlete. He became a hurdler at the age of sixteen, and at eighteen he won the World University Games in Beijing. In 2006 he broke the thirteen year-old world record for the 110-meter hurdles, and he has continued to win in international competitions. He is hugely popular in China, where his millions of fans follow his progress closely.

Olympic Games 2008

In August 2008, Beijing hosted the Olympic Games. More than 500 Chinese athletes competed in the Games. China's athletes are particularly successful in gymnastics, diving, and running.

Mah jong

In small villages in China, it is common to see people sitting outside around a table playing the ancient game of *mah jong*. In this game for four players, you try to build walls with tiles. A winning hand contains fourteen tiles.

Festivals and Holidays

The Chinese love festive celebrations. There are holidays and festivals all year round, but the most important is Chinese New Year.

Chinese New Year is a time of feasting with the family, celebrating, setting off fireworks, and giving gifts. Shops and offices close for three days, and millions of people travel to be with their family. The holiday begins on the first day of a new moon, and ends fifteen days later.

Dragon Boat Festival

During the Dragon Boat Festival in June, long decorated boats race on waterways to commemorate the death of the poet Chu Yuan, who drowned in 278 B.C.E. Rice dumplings are a traditional food for that day. The boats are about thirty feet long, with each end ornately carved and painted with dragons' heads and tails. They are manned by twenty or twenty-two paddlers.

DID YOU KNOW?
October 1st is National Day in China. It celebrates the founding of the People's Republic of China in 1949.

New Year customs

The whole family eats together on New Year's Eve, and they remember their **ancestors**. Children stay up late, and the next morning they give their parents good wishes. In return, they are given little red packets of *lai see*, or "lucky money." A parade takes place on the last day of the festival. Decorations are in red, because the Chinese believe it to be a lucky color.

Ching Ming and Chung Yeun

The Ching Ming and Chung Yeun festivals are when people pay respects to their ancestors. On these two occasions, the whole family gathers in front of their ancestors' graves.

Moon festival

This festival takes place during the eighth lunar month. People let off fireworks when the Moon appears, and eat special Moon cakes made with red beans, pastry, egg yolk, and black nuts. The Moon cakes represent Chang'e, the wife of Houyi, who lives on the Moon (see page 20).

Lion dance

The Chinese lion dance is about 2,000 years old. It is performed at Chinese New Year and other festivals. Two dancers are inside the costume, one for the head and one for the body and tail. Their energetic dance is accompanied by music.

Glossary

ancestors people who were members of your family a long time ago

autonomous regions areas with a certain amount of control over its own government

bronze metal that is a mixture of copper and tin

calligraphy form of decorative writing produced usually with a brush, but also with a pen

characters symbols for letters or sounds in Chinese writing

civil war fighting between two or more groups in the same country

communist person or something that is part of a political system where the state controls property, industry, and trade

Cultural Revolution movement by Chairman Mao to "purify" Chinese communism by imprisoning or killing many educated people

democracy system of government where people elect representatives to govern them

dynasties families that rule for several generations

endangered under threat of dying out completely

ethnic group group of people with the same culture or nationality

exile living in another country because you have been forced to leave your own country

hydroelectric producing electricity using the power of moving water

immigrants people who go to live in another country

immortals people who live forever

legislative body assembly that makes or changes a country's laws

martial arts traditional fighting sports such as Kung Fu and Tai Chi, used for self-defense or combat

plateau area of flat land that is higher than the surrounding land

republic country whose head of state is not a king or queen; usually governed by a president

rural in the countryside

Silk Road from about 100 B.C.E. to the fifteenth century C.E., an important overland trade route from China, through Central Asia to the Mediterranean Sea and Europe

terracotta brownish-red kind of pottery, Italian for "baked earth"

Find Out More

Books

Challen, Paul. *Life in Ancient China.*
  Crabtree Publishing Company, 2004

Goulding, Sylvia. *Festive Foods: China.*
  Chelsea Clubhouse, 2008

Kalman, Bobbie. *China: The Culture.*
  Crabtree Publishing Company, 2008

Kule, Elaine A. *Celebrate Chinese New Year.*
  Enslow Publishers, 2006

Pilon, Pascal, and Elisabeth Thomas. *Kids Around the World: We Live in China.*
  Abrams Books for Young Readers, 2006

Sebag-Montefiore, Hugh. *Eyewitness: China.* Dorling Kindersley, 2007

Shepard, Aaron. *Monkey: A Superhero Tale of China, Retold from The Journey to the West.* Skyhook, 2005

Web sites

http://www.cnto.org/aboutchina.asp
The official site of China's national tourist office is packed with useful information.

http://www.travelchinaguide.com/cityguides/
This site has very detailed information on China's growing cities and on the top sights to see in the country.

http://www.chineseart.com/chinese-painting.htm
Find out more about Chinese painting at this Web site.

http://www.chineseart.com/chinese-inventions-1.htm
Find out about Chinese inventions that changed the world at this site.

http://www.historyforkids.org/learn/china/
Explore China at this Web site especially for kids.

Index